Copyright @ 2024 FINEXTIFY

Written by Deo Sango

finextify.com

finextify.com / @finextify

TABLE OF CONTENTS

Introduction

Exploring the Strength of Community- Circles

In a world where financial security is often elusive and economic disparities continue to widen, the concept of community-based saving circles emerges as a beacon of hope and resilience. These circles, deeply ingrained in cultural traditions and social networks, represent a powerful tool for individuals and communities to navigate financial challenges and achieve shared prosperity. This introduction will delve into the significance of community-based saving circles, defining their essence, highlighting the importance of collective saving, and providing an overview of the book structure.

A. Defining Community-Based Saving Circles

Community-based saving circles, alternatively referred to as ROSCAs (Rotating Savings and Credit Associations), tandas, tontine, stokvel, or susus, represent informal financial arrangements in which a collective of individuals unite to pool their resources and save collectively. Each member contributes a fixed amount of money to the circle at regular intervals, and in turn, each member takes turns receiving the pooled funds. This cyclical process continues until all members have had the opportunity to receive a payout. These circles are not only about saving money but also about building trust, fostering social connections, and supporting one another financially.

B. Importance of Collective Saving

The importance of collective saving cannot be overstated, especially for individuals and communities facing financial constraints or limited access to formal banking services. By participating in community-based saving circles, individuals can overcome barriers to saving and access lump sums of money when needed. Furthermore, collective saving promotes financial discipline, encourages long-term saving habits, and provides a safety net during times of financial hardship. Beyond the financial benefits, these circles strengthen social bonds, foster a sense of solidarity, and empower participants to take control of their financial futures.

C. Overview of the book Structure

This ebook aims to explore the multifaceted nature of community-based saving circles, delving into their historical roots, cultural significance, psychological underpinnings, practical benefits, and prospects. Through a combination of theoretical insights, real-life case studies, and practical tips, readers will gain a comprehensive understanding of how these circles or group savings operate and their potential as transformative financial tools. The book is structured to provide a holistic view of community-based saving circles, covering their evolution, mechanics, benefits, challenges, and technological advancements. Each chapter offers valuable insights and actionable strategies for individuals and communities looking to harness the power of collective saving. Join us as we unlock the secrets of community-based saving circles and explore their profound impact on financial inclusion and resilience.

CHAPTER 2 : The Journey of Savings Circles

From Past to Present Solutions

A. Origins of Saving Circles

The origins of saving circles reach back to early human history, when communities worldwide practiced variations of collective saving to manage their finances and provide mutual support. While the exact origins remain uncertain, evidence suggest informal savings groups existed in varying forms across different cultures and societies throughout history. Ancient Egypt records community-based savings arrangements called "tontines" in which members contributed payments into a communal fund and received payouts at regular intervals. Similarly, in China, informal associations called "hui" sprang up pertaining to specific functions such as weddings or funerals.

In traditional societies, savings circles played key roles in resource-pooling, financial aid, and the bolstering of community ties. Operating within the milieu of reciprocity and trust, group members provided practical support to fellow members through collective savings and lending activities.

Savings circles have evolved over time in terms of their structure and function. Informal savings groups played a critical role for immigrant communities in countries such as the United States starting in the 19th and early 20th centuries as they were establishing themselves. These "sou-sou" and "tandas" are examples of some of the informal savings groups they created in order to pool their resources and build a financial foothold for themselves. These informal savings circles enabled new arrivals to access credit and understand the mechanics of life "across the line."

Savings circles have evolved in recent times as a result of technology and globalization. Access has been broadened and transactions have been simplified by digital platforms and mobile technology. As such, a broad range of savings circles — from longstanding community-based models to providers that rely strictly on digital platforms — now operate. Fast forward to the present day and we see that savings circles are further adapting in keeping with changes in financial practices and the growing influence of technology on financial inclusion initiatives.

CHAPTER 2

B. Cultural and Historical Significance

Savings circles hold great cultural and historical significance, embodying principles of cooperation and unity within communities. Across various cultures worldwide, they've served not only as financial tools but also as vital social and cultural institutions. These circles fostered mutual support during difficult times, marked communal achievements, and preserved cultural heritage through shared practices.

In many traditional societies, savings circles were fundamental to everyday life, allowing people to pool resources, redistribute wealth, and assist each other when needed. Rooted in cultural traditions and community values, participants collaborated to tackle financial challenges together.

For instance, in African and Caribbean cultures, savings circles like "susu" or "sou-sous" were essential lifelines during economic struggles, strengthening social ties and solidarity. Similarly, in Asian cultures, "hui" or "chit funds" supported savings, major expenses, and entrepreneurial endeavors, empowering individuals to reach their financial objectives.

Throughout history, savings circles empowered marginalized groups, especially women, by offering access to financial services and economic opportunities. As societies modernize, these circles evolve by embracing digital platforms while preserving their cultural and historical importance, reflecting the enduring traditions of communities worldwide.

C. Evolution into Modern Community-Based Saving Models

As societies evolved and economies became more complex, the concept of saving circles adapted to meet the changing needs of communities. In the 19th and early 20th centuries, immigrant communities in the United States established informal savings and lending clubs, such as "tandas" or "sousou," to support one another financially and maintain cultural ties. These clubs provided a sense of belonging and solidarity in a new and unfamiliar environment, helping immigrants navigate the challenges of assimilation and economic hardship.

In recent times, the evolution of savings circles has led to the development of more organized and structured models, often referred to as rotating savings and credit associations (ROSCAs) or stokvels (South Africa). These entities function on a rotational basis, with participants contributing fixed sums of money at consistent intervals and then alternating in receiving the pooled funds. The emergence of technology has further simplified participation in savings circles, with digital platforms and mobile applications enabling individuals to join from anywhere globally, thus facilitating smooth transactions.

CHAPTER 2

D. Importance of Community-Based Saving

The importance of community-based saving lies in its ability to promote financial inclusion, resilience, and empowerment, particularly among underserved and marginalized communities. By pooling resources and sharing financial risks, savings circles enable individuals to access capital, build assets, and achieve financial goals that might otherwise be out of reach. Moreover, savings circles foster a sense of community ownership and control over financial resources, empowering participants to take control of their economic destinies and improve their quality of life.

In summary, the history and evolution of savings circles underscore the enduring relevance and importance of collective saving and community solidarity in addressing economic challenges and promoting financial well-being. From their ancient origins to their modern iterations, savings circles continue to serve as powerful tools for building wealth, fostering social cohesion, and creating a more equitable and sustainable future for all.

CHAPTER 3 : The Psychology of Saving

Exploring How Community Circles Drive Financial Choice

Understanding the psychological factors that underpin saving behavior is crucial in comprehending the effectiveness of community-based saving circles. By delving into behavioral economics, social influence, and motivation, we can unravel the intricate dynamics that drive individuals to participate in these circles and maintain their commitment to saving collectively.

A. Behavioral Economics and Saving Habits

Behavioral economics offers valuable insights into how individuals make financial decisions and the cognitive biases that influence their saving habits. While traditional economic theory assumes rational decision-making based on preferences and available information, behavioral economics recognizes the impact of psychological factors like cognitive biases, emotions, and social norms. In the realm of saving circles, these insights help explain why individuals may choose to participate despite potential drawbacks, such as delayed gratification or loss aversion.

Bounded rationality is a key concept in behavioral economics, suggesting that individuals make decisions with limited information and cognitive abilities. This limitation often leads to behaviors like procrastination, impulsivity, or present bias, where immediate gratification takes precedence over long-term savings goals. Cognitive biases further shape saving habits; mental accounting, for instance, leads individuals to allocate funds based on arbitrary criteria rather than maximizing overall utility, impacting decisions related to emergency funds or retirement savings.

Loss aversion is another cognitive bias affecting saving behavior, causing individuals to prefer avoiding losses over acquiring equivalent gains. This aversion may deter them from taking risks or investing in opportunities with higher returns, even if financially prudent. Understanding these biases is crucial in the context of saving circles, where participants may face uncertainty about future returns or the need for delayed gratification.

Moreover, behavioral economics highlights the role of framing and context in influencing saving behavior. Positive reinforcement, incentives, and perceived social norms can motivate individuals to save, especially within community-based saving circles. The social aspect fosters a sense of belonging and obligation, encouraging participation and contributing to the group's goals.

In conclusion, behavioral economics provides insights into the psychological drivers of saving behavior and the effectiveness of community-based saving circles. By acknowledging and addressing cognitive biases, interventions and strategies can be designed to promote positive saving habits and enhance financial well-being among participants.

CHAPTER 3

B. Social Influence and Peer Pressure

Humans are naturally social creatures, meaning our actions and decisions are often influenced by those around us. When it comes to saving circles, social influence refers to how the behavior and expectations of group members can impact an individual's saving choices. Seeing others in the group actively participating and meeting saving goals can motivate individuals to join in the effort.

Peer pressure, a type of social influence, also plays a big role in shaping financial behavior within saving circles. It's when people feel pressure from their peers to act a certain way, pushing them to follow the group's norms. In saving circles, this might mean encouraging members to contribute regularly or stick to the group's rules.

Social proof is another way peer pressure affects saving behavior. When individuals see their peers successfully saving and benefiting from it, they're more likely to see saving as a positive action and want to join in. Fear of being left out or judged by the group can also push people to contribute, even if they weren't initially keen.

The connections and bonds within saving circles make social influence even stronger. Feeling part of a team and having support from peers can motivate members to stay committed to saving together. This sense of belonging and mutual support can inspire individuals to overcome challenges and stay focused on the group's financial goals.

In summary, social influence and peer pressure are powerful forces in driving saving behavior within saving circles. By understanding and embracing these dynamics, we can encourage positive saving habits and create a stronger, more prosperous future for everyone involved.

CHAPTER 3

C. Motivation and Accountability in Group Saving

Motivation and accountability are key ingredients that keep individuals engaged in group-saving initiatives. Motivation comes from different places, like wanting to reach financial goals, supporting the community, or following social norms. In saving circles, people feel driven to contribute regularly to keep up with the group and not disappoint their friends. Plus, the sense of responsibility that comes with being part of a collective effort strengthens saving habits and helps everyone stay committed to their goals.

Understanding why people join community-based saving circles and how these groups encourage positive financial behavior involves looking at a mix of thoughts, feelings, and social connections. Motivation is like the fuel that keeps the saving circle engine running. It can come from wanting to achieve security, help out friends, or just fit in with what others are doing. When you're in a saving circle, you're part of a team working together to save and invest for everyone's benefit. Feeling like you're in it together with your friends can really boost your motivation to save regularly and stick to the group's plans.

And then there's accountability, which is like having a teammate who's counting on you. Being in a saving circle means you've got a responsibility to your friends to keep up your end of the bargain. The group's rules and schedules help keep everyone on track, making sure everyone's doing their part and following through with their promises. Knowing that your friends are relying on you can give you that extra push to keep saving, even when it's tough.

In short, motivation and accountability are like the secret sauce that makes community-based saving circles work. They keep everyone focused on their goals, help build stronger bonds between friends, and make sure everyone's doing their fair share to reach financial success together.

CHAPTER 4 : How to Start and Join a Saving Circle

Step-by-Step Guide for Success

Starting and joining a savings circle can be a transformative step towards achieving your financial goals and building a strong sense of community. Whether you're looking to save for a specific purpose, such as a down payment on a house or a dream vacation, or simply want to cultivate better saving habits, a savings circle can provide the structure, support, and motivation needed to succeed. In this guide, we'll walk you through the process of initiating and joining a savings circle, step by step.

A. Initiating a Saving Circle

1. Define Your Goals: Before starting a savings circle, it's important to know what you're saving for. Whether it's a fun trip with friends or planning for the future, having clear goals helps shape your circle's focus.

2. Find Members: Look for friends, family, or coworkers who share your saving goals. Pick people you trust and who are reliable. Having a diverse group with different backgrounds can make your saving circle more interesting.

3. Create Guidelines: Get together with your potential members to decide how your circle will work. Figure out things like how much everyone will contribute and how often payouts will happen. Having clear rules makes sure everyone knows what to expect.

4. Stay Connected: Communication is key! Set up a chat or email group where you can all talk about your circle. This way, you can keep track of contributions and talk about any problems that come up.

5. Choose a Platform: Decide how you'll handle contributions and payouts. You can use a bank account, a payment app, or even just keep track manually. Just make sure everyone knows how it works.

6. Make it Official: Before you get started, write down all the rules and agreements in a document. This makes sure everyone is on the same page and committed to the circle's goals.

Following these steps can help you start a savings circle with your friends and work towards your financial goals together. Remember, it's not just about saving money—it's also about supporting each other and building a strong community. With everyone pitching in and communicating openly, your savings circle can help you achieve your dreams and build a brighter future.

CHAPTER 4

B. Establishing Rules and Guidelines

Starting or joining a savings circle can be a great way to save money and build a supportive community. Whether you're saving up for something special or just want to get better at saving, a savings circle can give you the structure and motivation you need to reach your goals. In this guide, we'll go through the steps of starting or joining a savings circle, focusing on setting up rules and guidelines for success.

1. Define the Purpose: First, figure out what you want your savings circle to achieve. Are you saving for a specific goal, like a trip or a new gadget? Or maybe you just want to build up an emergency fund. Knowing your purpose will help you set rules that fit your group's goals.

2. Set Contribution Parameters: Decide how often and how much everyone will contribute to the savings pool. This could be weekly, bi-weekly, or monthly, depending on what works best for your group. Make sure the contributions are fair and affordable for everyone.

3. Establish a Rotation System: Decide how you'll distribute the pooled funds to members. You could take turns receiving the money, or you could use an auction-style system where members bid for their turn. Choose a system that's fair and works for everyone.

4. Define Withdrawal Rules: Decide when members can take money out of the savings pool and under what circumstances. Make sure everyone knows the rules to avoid any confusion or disagreements later on.

5. Establish Accountability Measures: Find ways to make sure everyone sticks to the rules. This could mean checking in regularly, tracking progress, or keeping an eye on each other's contributions. Open communication and trust are key.

6. Document Rules and Guidelines: Write down all the rules and guidelines in a formal agreement that everyone can agree to. Include everything from the purpose of the savings circle to how withdrawals will work. Having everything in writing can help avoid misunderstandings later on.

By following these steps and working together, you can create a successful savings circle that helps everyone reach their financial goals. With clear rules and good communication, you'll be well on your way to saving money and supporting each other along the way.

CHAPTER 4

C. Joining Existing Circles

Joining a savings circle can be a game-changer for reaching your financial goals and connecting with others in your community. Whether you're saving up for something special or just want to develop better money habits, a savings circle can give you the structure and encouragement you need to succeed. In this guide, we'll walk you through the process of joining an existing savings circle, step by step.

1. Find Potential Circles: Start by looking for savings circles that match your goals and values. You can ask friends, family, or coworkers if they know of any circles you could join, or you can search online for groups in your community.

2. Ask About Openings: Once you've found some potential circles, reach out to the members or organizers to see if they have any openings. Let them know you're interested in joining and ask about the process for becoming a member.

3. Attend Meetings: If possible, attend a meeting or discussion of the savings circle to learn more about how it works and who's involved. This will give you a chance to ask questions and make sure it's a good fit for you.

4. Review the Rules: Before you commit to joining a circle, make sure you understand and agree with the rules and guidelines. Pay attention to things like how much you'll need to contribute and how payouts are handled.

5. Show Your Commitment: Once you've decided to join a circle, let the other members know that you're committed to the group's goals and rules. Be reliable about making your contributions and following through on your commitments.

6. Get Involved: Once you're a member, be an active participant in the circle. Contribute regularly, participate in discussions, and support your fellow members. The more you put into the circle, the more you'll get out of it.

By following these steps, you'll be well on your way to joining a savings circle and working towards your financial goals. Remember to communicate openly, stay committed, and enjoy the support of your fellow members along the way.

CHAPTER 5 : The Advantages of Community Circles

Financial, Social, and Emotional benefits

Participating in community-based circles offers a multitude of benefits that extend beyond mere financial gains. These circles, rooted in collective efforts and mutual support, provide individuals with opportunities to enhance their financial well-being, foster social connections, and nurture emotional resilience.

A. Financial Benefits: Increased Savings, Lower Costs

Participating in community-based circles offers a range of financial benefits that can help individuals save money and improve their financial well-being. By pooling resources with other members, participants can increase their savings and reduce costs compared to saving alone. Regular contributions to the group fund build a substantial nest egg that can be used for emergencies, investments, or major expenses. Plus, pooling resources allows members to access larger sums of money without resorting to high-interest loans or credit cards, saving them from extra fees and charges. Collective purchasing power also means members can negotiate better deals and discounts, stretching their dollars further.

Beyond financial perks, community-based circles provide valuable opportunities for learning and growth. Members can access financial education resources and learn essential money management skills through workshops and peer-to-peer knowledge sharing. This knowledge empowers individuals to make informed decisions, build wealth, and achieve their long-term financial goals.

Apart from financial benefits, participating in these circles offers social advantages too. Members can connect with like-minded peers, build meaningful relationships, and feel a sense of belonging and support within the community. The social aspect fosters a supportive environment where members can share experiences, offer advice, and celebrate achievements together. These interactions provide emotional support and encouragement during challenging times, enriching members' social lives and strengthening their connections.

Additionally, participating in community-based circles broadens individuals' social networks and exposes them to diverse perspectives and opportunities. Interacting with people from different backgrounds expands horizons, fosters learning, and enriches life experiences.

Moreover, these circles offer significant emotional advantages. They provide a supportive space where members can express themselves, share struggles, and receive empathy and understanding from others. This emotional support helps individuals navigate challenges, cope with stress, and build resilience. It also boosts self-esteem, confidence, and sense of self-worth, empowering members to reach their full potential and enhance their overall well-being.

CHAPTER 5

B. Social Benefits: Building Trust, Strengthening Relationships

Engaging in community-based circles offers numerous benefits that extend beyond just financial gains. These circles, grounded in collective efforts and mutual support, provide avenues for improving financial well-being, nurturing social connections, and bolstering emotional resilience.

One of the key social advantages of being part of community-based circles is the chance to build trust and form strong relationships with others. Within these circles, members interact, collaborate, and forge meaningful connections based on shared goals and values.

Trust is a crucial component within these circles, as it encourages cooperation, communication, and teamwork among members. As individuals contribute to the collective effort and witness the dedication of their peers, trust grows, laying a sturdy foundation for mutual support and joint endeavors.

Moreover, participating in community-based circles offers opportunities to strengthen existing relationships and cultivate new connections with like-minded individuals. Through shared activities and discussions, members develop bonds of friendship and camaraderie that extend beyond the circle's boundaries, providing companionship and support.

Additionally, these circles promote inclusivity and diversity by bringing together people from various backgrounds and perspectives. Interacting with individuals of diverse viewpoints fosters empathy, tolerance, and respect, creating an environment of acceptance and inclusion within the circle.

Furthermore, collaboration and teamwork are encouraged within community-based circles, allowing members to achieve greater success collectively than they could alone. By combining resources, sharing ideas, and leveraging each other's strengths, members foster unity and solidarity, reinforcing trust and deepening relationships.

In summary, the social benefits of participating in community-based circles are profound, enriching individuals' lives and strengthening their social connections. Through active engagement, members can develop meaningful relationships, expand their networks, and experience the support and camaraderie of a welcoming community.

CHAPTER 5

C. Emotional Benefits: Support System, Sense of Belonging

Joining community-based circles offers more than just financial gains; it's about building connections and resilience. These circles provide a supportive environment where you can share your feelings and experiences, receiving empathy and understanding from others.

Being part of such a circle is like having a safety net for life's challenges. Whether you're dealing with money problems, personal setbacks, or tough emotions, your circle mates are there to offer advice, encouragement, and a shoulder to lean on.

Plus, being in a community circle helps forge deep friendships beyond just hanging out. You bond through shared activities and chats, creating a place where everyone feels valued and accepted.

These circles also celebrate diversity, welcoming people from different backgrounds. Meeting folks with various viewpoints broadens your understanding and teaches empathy and respect for others.

Engaging in community circles isn't just about being social; it's about growing as a person. Achieving goals together boosts confidence and happiness, making you feel fulfilled and purposeful.

Ultimately, community circles provide a supportive space where you can find comfort, friendship, and a sense of belonging, helping you navigate life's ups and downs with confidence and resilience.

CHAPTER 6 : Real-Life Success Stories

Examples of Community Saving Circles in Action

Community-based savings circles have demonstrated their efficacy as instruments for nurturing financial resilience, promoting social cohesion, and empowering individuals to reach their financial objectives. Through real-life case studies, we can gain insights into how these circles operate, the challenges they face, and the impact they have on participants' lives. In this section, we explore various success stories of community-based saving circles and examine the factors contributing to their success.

.

A. Case Study 1: Saving Circle Success Story in a Rural Community

Imagine a beautiful rural area with rolling hills and green fields where a group of women decided to team up and form the "Saheli Savings Group." This circle included ten women with different backgrounds like farmers, artists, and small business owners, all sharing a common goal: to improve their finances and support each other.

They met every month at someone's house, bringing their savings together and chatting about money stuff like budgeting, investing, and starting businesses. Each member put in a certain amount of money, which they used to help each other out with loans or invest in things that would benefit everyone.

What made this group really work was how they welcomed everyone and worked as a team. Even though they faced doubts and cultural differences at first, they stuck together, building trust and creating a supportive atmosphere where everyone felt valued. By embracing their unique strengths and working together, they made incredible progress.

Thanks to their teamwork, the Saheli Savings Group achieved some big financial goals, like starting new businesses, expanding farms, and making sure their kids could go to school. They also invested in things like organic farming and crafts, which didn't just help them individually but boosted the whole community's economy.

But it wasn't just about money. This group was also a place where these women could become leaders, stand up for their rights, and challenge old ideas about gender. By taking part in decisions and leading roles, they grew more confident and took control of their lives.

In short, the Saheli Savings Group shows how coming together in savings circles can make a real difference in rural areas. By working together, trusting each other, and empowering one another, they showed that anything is possible, even in tough times, helping everyone build a brighter future.

CHAPTER 6

B. Case Study 2: Urban Saving Transforming Financial Futures

Imagine a bustling city where a group of young professionals, freelancers, and entrepreneurs came together to form a saving circle called "CitySavers." Their goal? To shape their financial destinies in the fast-paced urban world they lived in. CitySavers was all about building savings, investing wisely, and backing each other up in the urban jungle.

They met up regularly at local cafes or community hubs to chat about money matters, share tips, and cheer each other on. What made CitySavers special was its flexible approach. Members could pitch in whatever they could afford, based on their own goals and finances. Their contributions went into a pot that was used to give loans to members for business ventures, education, or unexpected expenses.

A big reason behind CitySavers' success was how they embraced technology. They knew city life came with its own set of challenges, like high costs and job uncertainties. So, they used digital tools and online platforms to stay connected, keep track of their savings, and make transactions. This made everything smoother and more accessible for everyone involved.

Thanks to CitySavers, members achieved some awesome financial goals, like starting businesses, advancing their education, and building up emergency funds. The circle's supportive vibe and lending system gave members access to money and resources they might not have had otherwise, helping them chase their dreams and break down financial barriers.

But CitySavers wasn't just about money. It also opened doors for personal and professional growth. By mingling with folks from different backgrounds and industries, members expanded their networks, learned new skills, and got valuable advice that boosted their careers and personal lives.

In a nutshell, CitySavers showed how saving circles in cities can make a real difference. By teaming up, being innovative, and supporting one another, they proved that even in the fast-paced urban grind, you can take control of your finances and thrive.

CHAPTER 6

C. Case Study 3: Cultural Saving Circle Traditions Around the World

Community-based saving circles have become vital tools for building financial strength, unity among people, and economic empowerment. By looking at real-life examples, we can see how these circles work, what they mean culturally, and how they change lives. Let's explore some success stories from different parts of the world and see how cultural traditions shape them.

In many cultures, saving circles are a cornerstone of community life, offering support, preserving culture, and ensuring financial stability. For instance, in West Africa, there's the "susu" or "Tontine" tradition, where people form informal groups to save money together. Each member contributes regularly, and then, in turn, receives a lump sum, helping with starting businesses or supporting family needs.

In Latin America, the "tanda" tradition is common, where individuals pool money and one member receives the total sum each cycle. This helps with expenses like education or healthcare without relying on high-interest loans.

In Asia, like in India, the "chit fund" system is popular. Here, people pool money, and through auctions, distribute it among members. This helps with big expenses like weddings or education fees.

These traditions show how people worldwide come together, support each other, and achieve goals through teamwork. By relying on community ties and trust, these circles help individuals overcome financial hurdles and preserve cultural practices for the future. They're a testament to communities' resilience and creativity in navigating modern challenges while keeping their heritage alive.

CHAPTER 7 : Navigating Challenges

Common Obstacles and Solutions in Community Saving Circles

While community-based saving circles offer numerous benefits, they also face various challenges that can hinder their effectiveness and sustainability. By understanding these challenges and implementing appropriate solutions, participants can overcome obstacles and ensure the success of their saving circles. In this section, we explore common obstacles and solutions in community-based saving circles, focusing on the challenge of "Lack of Trust and Accountability."

A. Lack of Trust and Accountability

One major hurdle for community-based saving circles is the issue of trust and accountability among members. Some people may hesitate to join these circles because they worry about whether others will follow through on their commitments or if the group will manage funds responsibly. Without trust and accountability, these circles can struggle to attract and keep members engaged, which can lead to problems and disinterest within the group.

One solution to this challenge is setting up clear rules and guidelines for how the saving circle operates. By establishing expectations about contributions, withdrawals, and decision-making, everyone knows what's expected, promoting transparency and accountability. Having trusted individuals oversee the circle's management and enforce these rules can also help keep things orderly and prevent conflicts.

Encouraging open communication is crucial too. Regular meetings and discussions allow members to share concerns, resolve issues, and work together on solutions, fostering a culture of transparency and collaboration that builds trust.

Implementing monitoring tools, like digital platforms, can also enhance accountability by tracking contributions and withdrawals in real-time. This transparency not only prevents fraud but also gives members confidence in the circle's integrity.

In summary, building trust and accountability is key to the success of community-based saving circles. Clear rules, open communication, and monitoring mechanisms can help overcome these challenges, allowing members to work together effectively towards their financial goals.

CHAPTER 7

B. Unequal Participation and Contributions

Community-based saving circles are fantastic for building financial strength, unity, and empowerment. But, like any group effort, they come with challenges. Let's zoom in on one biggie: "Unequal Participation and Contributions."

One of the toughest hurdles for saving circles is when some members chip in more than others, creating an imbalance in benefits. This can stir up bad vibes like tension and resentment among members, putting a damper on the circle's vibe.

So, how do we tackle this? First off, clear rules and expectations help everyone understand their role. Setting a minimum contribution ensures fairness, giving everyone a fair shot at reaping the rewards.

Transparency is also key. Keeping accurate records lets members track their progress and holds everyone accountable for their part. Plus, regular chats help air out concerns and find solutions as a team.

Furthermore, saving circles can implement mechanisms to incentivize equal participation and contributions among members. For example, offering rewards or incentives for consistent participation or providing opportunities for members to earn additional benefits through active engagement can motivate individuals to contribute more actively to the group. By aligning incentives with desired behaviors, saving circles can encourage greater involvement and commitment from all members, fostering a sense of ownership and shared responsibility.

To sweeten the deal, circles can offer perks for active involvement, like bonuses or extra benefits. By making sure everyone feels valued and included, saving circles can thrive, paving the way for success and prosperity for all.

In conclusion, addressing the challenge of unequal participation and contributions is essential for the success and sustainability of community-based saving circles. By promoting fairness, transparency, and accountability, saving circles can create an inclusive and supportive environment where all members have an equal opportunity to thrive. Through collaborative efforts and mutual support, participants can overcome obstacles and achieve their financial goals collectively, strengthening the bonds of the community and fostering long-term prosperity for all.

CHAPTER 7

C. Handling Disputes and Issues

Community-based saving circles are awesome for boosting finances and forging friendships, but sometimes, bumps in the road pop up. Let's chat about one of these hurdles: "Handling Disputes and Issues."

A big challenge for saving circles is when disagreements or problems crop up among members. Maybe there's confusion about the rules, or folks have different ideas about how things should run. If these issues aren't sorted out, they can lead to tension and even break up the circle.

So, what's the game plan? First off, clear communication is key. Having a way to talk about problems openly and respectfully can make a huge difference. It helps to have someone neutral, like a mediator, to help folks work things out calmly.

Building a culture of respect and understanding is super important too. When everyone feels valued and heard, it's easier to find common ground and sort out issues peacefully. Encouraging folks to listen to each other and approach disagreements with empathy can lead to positive solutions.

Furthermore, saving circles can establish clear rules, guidelines, and procedures for handling disputes and issues, ensuring that all members understand their rights and responsibilities. By outlining the steps for addressing grievances, resolving conflicts, and appealing decisions, saving circles can provide clarity and consistency in the dispute resolution process, reducing ambiguity and minimizing the risk of escalation.

Setting up clear rules for handling disputes is also smart. Knowing what to do if things get rocky helps keep everyone on the same page and avoids confusion. By working together and sticking to shared values, saving circles can overcome challenges and keep the good vibes flowing.

CHAPTER 8 : Using Technology

Improving Community Saving Circles with Digital Platform

In the contemporary digital era, technology assumes a vital role in revolutionizing how we save, invest, and handle our finances. Community-based saving circles have also embraced technology, leveraging digital platforms to enhance their operations, increase efficiency, and improve accessibility for participants. In this section, we explore how digital platforms enhance community-based saving circles, with a focus on the introduction to digital saving platforms.

A. Introduction to Digital Saving Platforms

Digital saving platforms have changed the game for community-based saving circles, making it easier than ever for participants to handle their savings, contributions, and investments. These platforms are like all-in-one tools that make managing money a breeze.

One big perk of digital saving platforms is how they take care of boring tasks automatically. Stuff like keeping track of who's paid what, figuring out payouts, and making reports is all done in a snap. This means less time spent on paperwork and more time to focus on growing savings and making smart choices. Plus, with less chance of mistakes, everyone can trust that things are being done right.

These platforms also give participants a real-time look at their savings and investments. With cool features like interactive charts and personalized reports, it's easy to see how things are going and where there's room for improvement.

And the best part? Digital saving platforms bring people together, no matter where they are. Whether you're across town or across the globe, you can chat with fellow savers, share ideas, and work towards goals as a team. It's like having a financial support squad right at your fingertips.

In short, digital saving platforms have made community-based saving circles even better by making saving and investing simpler, more efficient, and more connected than ever before. With technology on their side, saving circles can reach their goals faster and help everyone in the group thrive financially.

CHAPTER 8

B. Benefits of Technology in Saving Circles

In today's tech-savvy world, technology isn't just for scrolling through social media or playing games—it's also changing the way we handle our money. Even community-based saving circles, which used to rely on old-school methods like paper and pen, are getting a digital makeover. Let's dive into how technology is making saving circles even better!

Digital platforms are like superheroes for saving circles, making it way easier for everyone involved to save, invest, and work together towards their financial goals. One big plus of technology is how it takes care of boring tasks automatically. Stuff like keeping track of who's paid what, figuring out payouts, and making reports—all done in a snap. That means less time doing paperwork and more time focusing on growing savings and making smart choices.

Plus, digital platforms give participants a real-time look at their savings and investments. With cool features like interactive charts and personalized reports, it's easy to see how things are going and where there's room for improvement. And because everything's online, it's super easy to chat with other savers, share ideas, and work together as a team—whether you're across town or across the globe.

But it's not just about convenience—technology also makes saving circles safer and more secure. With fancy encryption and other high-tech security measures, your financial info stays safe from prying eyes, giving everyone peace of mind.

So, thanks to technology, saving circles are becoming more efficient, accessible, and connected than ever before. With digital platforms by their side, saving circles can reach their goals faster and help everyone in the group thrive financially.

CHAPTER 8

C. Popular Saving Apps and Platforms

In the world of community-based saving circles, technology is like a superpower, making everything easier and more fun! Digital platforms, like saving apps and websites, have changed the game, making it way easier for people to save money together and reach their financial goals.

One awesome app is called Paybash (To be launched soon). With Paybash or Heapin, you can create or join saving circles with your friends, family, or even coworkers. It's like a digital piggy bank where everyone chips in, and you can track your progress toward your savings goals together. Plus, you can chat with your circle members right in the app, so it's easy to stay connected and motivated!

Another cool app is Qapital. Qapital lets you set up personalized savings goals and then saves money for you automatically. You can set it to save a little bit every time you buy something, or even based on certain actions or events. It's like having a super-smart piggy bank that helps you save money without even thinking about it!

And if you're ready to take your savings to the next level, apps like Stash and Acorns let you invest your money in stocks and bonds, even if you're just starting out. They make investing easy and fun, with helpful tips and advice along the way.

Plus, apps like Heapin and Discord are great for staying in touch with your saving circle buddies. You can chat, share ideas, and even coordinate group activities—all from your phone or computer!

In conclusion, popular saving apps and platforms have revolutionized the way community-based saving circles operate, offering participants a wide range of tools and functionalities to manage their savings, investments, and communication with greater efficiency and convenience. By leveraging technology, saving circles can overcome geographical barriers, streamline administrative tasks, and foster collaboration and engagement among participants, ultimately empowering them to achieve their financial goals and aspirations collectively.

CHAPTER 9 : Optimizing Investments

Using Community-Based Circles for Smart Investing

Community-based saving circles offer participants not only a means to save money collectively but also an opportunity to invest and grow their savings. By pooling resources and leveraging collective purchasing power, participants can access a wide range of investment opportunities that may otherwise be out of reach as individuals. In this section, we explore strategies for using community-based circles as an investment tool, starting with an introduction to investment opportunities.

A. Introduction to Investment Opportunities

Community-based saving circles are awesome because they open up a world of investment possibilities! You've got your traditional stuff like stocks and bonds, but also some cool alternative options like real estate, commodities, and peer-to-peer lending.

Let's start with the stock market. It's like a big playground where you can invest in companies and potentially make money as they grow. With saving circles, you can pool your money together and invest in things called ETFs or mutual funds. These spread your money out across lots of different companies, which helps lower the risk and could lead to bigger returns over time.

Then there's real estate. You can invest in houses or buildings directly, or through things like REITs or crowdfunding platforms. Real estate can be neat because you can make money from renting out properties or selling them later when they've gone up in value.

Ever heard of peer-to-peer lending? It's like being the bank! You lend money to people or small businesses through platforms and earn interest in return. Just be sure to understand the risks involved.

Lastly, there's socially responsible investing. This is where you invest in companies that are doing good things for the world, like helping the environment or treating their workers well. It's like making money while making a positive impact!

So, with all these options, saving circles can help us grow our money and achieve our financial goals. Pretty cool, right? By working together and making smart choices, we can all build a brighter financial future!

CHAPTER 9

B. Educating Saving Circle Members about Investment Options

Community-based saving circles aren't just about saving money together; they're also about growing our savings through smart investments! But to make the most of these investment opportunities, all circle members need to understand their options. Let's explore some ways to educate everyone about investing!

First things first, we need to teach everyone about the different investment options out there. Some folks might not know much about investing or might feel unsure about it. So, we'll start by giving them the basics, like what different types of investments are, how they work, and what risks and rewards come with them.

One cool way to do this is by holding workshops, seminars, or webinars. These sessions can cover topics like different types of investments, how to spread out your money to lower risks and strategies for making smart investment decisions. By giving everyone a solid foundation in investing, we can help them feel more confident about exploring their options.

We can also provide resources like articles, videos, podcasts, and online courses to help people learn at their own pace. And having a library or online platform where folks can access these materials anytime can make learning even easier.

Bringing in guest speakers who are experts in investing can also be super helpful. They can share their knowledge and answer questions, giving everyone a deeper understanding of investing.

And for some hands-on learning, we can try out investment simulations or virtual trading platforms. These let people practice investing without risking real money, so they can learn by doing!

By educating everyone about investing, we can help them make smarter decisions, grow their savings, and reach their financial goals together. Learning together is the key to success!

CHAPTER 9

C. Diversifying Investments for Long-Term Growth

Community-based saving circles offer a fantastic chance for people to save and invest together, aiming for long-term growth. One crucial strategy for making the most of these investments is diversification, which means spreading our money across different types of investments. Let's take a closer look at why diversification is so important and how we can achieve sustained growth through it.

Diversification is like having a safety net for our investments. It means not putting all our eggs in one basket but spreading them out among various types of investments, like stocks, bonds, real estate, and other options. This way, if one part of our investment portfolio isn't doing well, the others can help balance it out.

Within each type of investment, like stocks or real estate, we can diversify even further. For example, in the stock market, we can invest in different industries like technology, healthcare, or finance. By spreading our investments across different sectors, we reduce the risk of losing money if one sector has problems while still having the chance to benefit if others do well.

However, it's important to be careful with alternative investments, like peer-to-peer lending or cryptocurrencies, as they can be riskier and more complex. To keep our investments on track, we should regularly check and adjust our portfolio to make sure it still matches our goals and risk tolerance. This way, we can maximize our chances of success and grow our savings over time!

In conclusion, diversifying investments for long-term growth is essential for maximizing returns and mitigating risk within community-based saving circles. By diversifying investments across various asset classes, industries, and geographic regions, individuals can construct a robust investment portfolio capable of enduring market fluctuations and generating consistent returns over time. Through strategic diversification, saving circle members can achieve their financial goals and aspirations while minimizing the impact of unforeseen events and market volatility on their investment portfolios.

CHAPTER 10 : The Future of Community Circles

Innovations, Trends, and Opportunities

As community-based saving circles continue to evolve and adapt to changing financial landscapes, the future holds a myriad of innovations, trends, and opportunities for participants to explore. In this section, we delve into the emerging trends in community-based saving circles and how they are shaping the future of collaborative saving and investment.

A. Emerging Trends in Community-Based Saving Circles

A cool new trend in community-based saving circles is using technology to make things easier and more transparent. With apps and digital platforms, people can now manage their savings and investments right from their phones! These tools let them set up automatic contributions, keep track of their money in real-time, and chat securely with other members. This makes it super easy for everyone to work together and reach their financial goals.

Another exciting trend is social impact investing, where people put their money into projects that make a positive difference in the world. Instead of just thinking about making money, they also want to help things like renewable energy or affordable housing. It's like making money while doing good!

There's also this cool idea of collaborative investment platforms. These platforms let people team up and invest in different things together, like real estate or startups. By pooling their resources, they can invest in stuff they couldn't afford on their own and get better returns.

And guess what? There's this new thing called decentralized finance (DeFi) and blockchain technology. It's like having a super secure and transparent way to manage money and investments without needing a bank or other middlemen. With DeFi, everyone can access financial services and products easily and without any hassle.

In conclusion, the future of community-based saving circles is filled with innovations, trends, and opportunities that promise to transform the way participants save, invest, and collaborate toward their financial goals. By embracing technology, social impact investing, collaborative investment platforms, and decentralized finance, community-based saving circles can unlock new avenues for growth, prosperity, and positive social change. As participants continue to adapt and innovate, community-based saving circles will remain a powerful tool for collective empowerment, financial resilience, and economic inclusion in the years to come.

CHAPTER 10

B. Potential Impact of Technology and Innovation

Looking into the future, community-based saving circles hold a lot of exciting potential. Innovations and new trends in finance are shaping what these circles can do, and technology is playing a big role in that.

Imagine being able to manage your savings and investments right from your phone! Digital platforms and mobile apps are making that possible. They let you set up automatic contributions, track your money in real time, and chat securely with other members of your saving circle. This makes it super easy to work together and reach your financial goals.

But that's not all. There's this thing called FinTech, which stands for financial technology. It's like using cool apps and services to do all sorts of financial stuff without needing a traditional bank. With FinTech, you can use things like peer-to-peer lending platforms or digital wallets to save, invest, and spend your money in new and exciting ways.

And get this - artificial intelligence (AI) and machine learning (ML) are helping people make smarter investment decisions. These technologies can analyze lots of financial data, spot trends, and give predictions. That means you can make better choices about where to invest your money and how to grow your savings over time.

In conclusion, the potential impact of technology and innovation on the future of community-based saving circles is significant, offering participants new opportunities to save, invest, and collaborate toward their financial goals. By embracing digital platforms, FinTech solutions, blockchain technology, and AI-powered algorithms, community-based saving circles can unlock new avenues for growth, prosperity, and financial inclusion. As technology continues to evolve and innovate, community-based saving circles will remain at the forefront of empowering participants to achieve financial resilience and prosperity collectively.

CHAPTER 10

C. Opportunities for Credit Building, Collaboration, and Growth

The future of community-based saving circles is bright, filled with exciting innovations and opportunities that can change how we save, invest, and work together toward financial goals. One big opportunity lies in credit building, which is super important for getting things like loans or credit cards. Normally, if you don't have much of a credit history, it's tough to get these things. But with community-based saving circles, you can show you're responsible with money by regularly saving, which can boost your chances of getting credit in the future.

Another cool thing about these circles is how they encourage collaboration. By joining forces with others, you can pool your savings, invest in things that make money, and even start your own business together. It's like having a team that helps you reach your financial goals faster and opens up new opportunities for making money.

And it's not just about money - community-based saving circles also offer chances for personal and professional growth. You can meet new people, learn new skills, and get advice from others who have been successful with their finances. Plus, by working together, you can make a positive impact on your community by investing in local projects or businesses, creating jobs, and helping others in need.

In conclusion, the opportunities for credit building, collaboration, and growth within community-based saving circles are vast and transformative. By leveraging collective resources, expertise, and networks, participants can strengthen their financial standing, pursue shared goals, and drive positive change in their communities. As community-based saving circles continue to evolve and innovate, they will remain powerful vehicles for empowerment, collaboration, and economic prosperity for participants and communities alike.

Conclusion

In wrapping up our exploration of community-based saving circles, it's clear these age-old traditions offer a lot when it comes to financial empowerment and bringing people together. From their humble beginnings to how they work today, saving circles have proven to be strong tools for saving together and supporting each other.

Throughout this book, we've looked at the history, psychology, mechanics, and benefits of community-based saving circles. We've seen how they've changed, from informal groups in ancient times to more organized setups. We've also learned about their cultural importance, showing how they help communities stick together and deal with money challenges.

We've also talked about why people join saving circles, like feeling influenced by friends or wanting to achieve goals together. Plus, we've given tips on how to start, join, and handle saving circles well. And we've highlighted all the good things that come from them, like feeling more secure financially and emotionally.

Looking forward, saving circles have a bright future, especially with new tech making it easier for more people to join in. By using digital tools and coming up with new ideas, we can make saving circles even better and help more people worldwide.

So, we invite you to try saving circles, whether you're joining one, starting one, or just spreading the word. By working together to save money, we can make money matters fairer for everyone and build a better future together. Come join us in discovering the wonder of community-based saving circles and creating a world where everyone can thrive!